Mel Bay Presents

Wedding Music for the Lever Harp

Twenty-three Classic, Traditional, and Ethnic Wedding Arrangements

*by Beth A. Kollé
and Laurie Riley*

MW00973067

CD CONTENTS

1 Carolan's Draught — Turlough O'Carolan [1:36]	13 Jesu, Joy of Man's Desiring — J.S. Bach [1:52]
2 Theme from 'Jupiter' — Gustav Holst [1:45]	14 March from 'Scipio' — G.F. Handel [1:55]
3 Celtic Prelude I (Kean O'Hara) — T. O'Carolan [1:25]	15 Searching for Lambs — Traditional [1:14]
4 Swedish Prelude (Kringellek från Gagnef) — Traditional [0:35]	16 Swedish Meditation (Sollerö Långdans) — Traditional [0:47]
5 Celtic Prelude II (Lady St. John) — T. O'Carolan [0:54]	17 Jewish Meditation (Ma Navu) — Traditional [1:22]
6 Jewish Wedding Song I (Tum-Balalayke) — Traditional [0:42]	18 Celtic Meditation (Eleanor Plunkett) — T. O'Carolan [2:35]
7 Jewish Wedding Song II (Zemer Lach) — Traditional [0:36]	19 Celtic Recessional I (Charles O'Conor) — T. O'Carolan [1:01]
8 St. Anthony Chorale — F. J. Haydn [2:34]	20 Celtic Recessional II (Frank Palmer) — T. O'Carolan [1:03]
9 Bridal Chorus — R. Wagner [1:33]	21 Celtic Recessional III (Gilliekrankie) — Traditional [0:37]
10 Canon in 'D' — J. Pachelbel [2:10]	22 The Royal Dream — Traditional [1:03]
11 Dance of the Blessed Spirits — C.W.R. von Gluck [1:32]	23 Trumpet Tune — H. Purcell [1:30]
12 Finale from 'Music for the Royal Fireworks' — G.F. Handel [0:50]	

1 2 3 4 5 6 7 8 9 0

Visit us on the Web at www.melbay.com — E-mail us at email@melbay.com

TABLE OF CONTENTS

Beth Kollé is well known for her performances in the duo Greensleeves, and as a founding member of the Celtic/Nordic group Stone Circle. She brings the richness of many cultures to her harp music, and to her flute-playing as well. She is one of very few vocalists performing in the traditional "kveding" style of folk-singing from Norway, and loves to bring to life the ancient ballads and songs of Scandinavia.

Beth has recorded, performed and taught Celtic and Nordic music in the United States and abroad, combining her skills as a multi-instrumentalist and vocalist with her fluency in Norwegian and knowledge of Nordic folk traditions. Beth holds a music degree from the University of Washington.

"Harp has enriched my life in a way that no other instrument has. There is a great reward that comes from watching others discover the beauty of the harp."

A professional musician since the age of ten, Laurie Riley has toured through-out the United States, in Canada and in Ireland. She plays selections from around the world and from historical times, as well as compositions of her own.

Laurie was instrumental in designing the modern double-strung harp, which has become popular in recent years among harpers. She has recorded eleven albums of harp music, authored five books, and made five instructional videos. She also judges harp competitions and teaches for harp organizations in the US and abroad.

"As a musician, I am gratefully aware that I hold in my hands the experience of music as a metaphor for life, which is offered as a gift to all who gather to listen."

Wedding Music for the Lever Harp

INTRODUCTION

This book contains a variety of classic, traditional, and ethnic music, some pieces you will recognize as "standards", and some you may never have heard before. Selections in this book may be played on any style or type of harp.

These tunes and pieces have been chosen because they are in the public domain (not owned by any company to which royalties have to be paid when they are played in public), and also because, in our experience, they make the difference between an ordinary wedding and a very special one.

This book is divided into sections: Preludes, Processionals, Meditations (pieces that can be used mid-ceremony), and Recessionals. Many of the pieces can also be used for receptions. Therefore, the music contained here can be more than enough to get you through an entire wedding ceremony and reception.

We have prepared the arrangements to be interesting to player and listener alike, and to take full advantage of the harmonic capabilities of the lever harp. Though we've avoided key modulations, there is an occasional passage where a lever must be flipped to attain accidentals. These are clearly indicated in the notation.

PLAYING FOR WEDDINGS

The harp is the quintessential wedding instrument. Its romantic image and sound make it ideal for the special day which represents a landmark in the life of the bride, the groom, and their families. The music they choose will stay with them in memory and meaning for a lifetime, no matter what their future holds. What a privilege it is to be a conduit for this gift of music.

HOW TO SELECT THE MUSIC

When you make arrangements to play for someone's wedding, they will either tell you what musical selections they want, or ask you what you can play. You have the option of being open to learning pieces they request, or giving them a list of your wedding repertoire from which to choose. Either way, it is important to agree on the tunes you will play before you sign your contract.

HOW MUCH TO CHARGE

What you can charge for your services is based upon your *skill level and experience*, and *how much time you spend in preparation with the bride or family*, as well as *how long you actually are present at the event*. It should also be based upon the going rate in your community. This last point is of prime importance, so we'll discuss this first.

Many harpists feel that they must charge less than others if they have less experience. However, this is not necessarily a good idea, as common courtesy of the business of weddings demands that you never undercut your fellow harpists' prices. Rather than another harpist being offended if you charge the same even though your skills are not at the same level (more skilled or less skilled, either way), they would be offended if you appear to be attempting to "steal the market" by setting your prices lower. (This is in direct contrast to performance fees for concerts, where the more skilled harpists charge more as an indication of their level of expertise.)

When you start playing for weddings, check with other harpists in your community and see what the going rate is. If there is no communication network yet developed among them, start one. Referrals are valuable. When you can't do a wedding or other event, you can give the client the name of another harpist, and the same will often be done for you. You can even do cooperative advertising with other harpists. There is always plenty of work to go around, and you may be surprised to find that instead of fighting over a few "gigs", you and your peers may find it a challenge to get all of them covered!

In any case, agree upon a going rate. Here's a sample rate chart (the figures below do not necessarily represent the going rate in your community, as rates vary in different areas):

·   Ceremony only: one hour or part thereof, no matter how many
    pieces you play $250

·   Reception only: same as above

·   Ceremony and Reception, 2 hours or less $350; 2 – 3 hours $400;
    3 – 4 hours $450

·   Rehearsal, 1 hour or part thereof $150; 1 – 2 hours $200

The amount of time for which you charge is the amount of time you are actually present; how long you play will be somewhat less than that. (I don't recommend *actually playing* more than 3 hours. You can injure yourself by playing too long. It's not worth any amount of money to deal with tendonitis and other repetitive stress syndromes.)

SKILL LEVEL

If you are a professional player, no doubt you've played many weddings. A confident intermediate or advanced amateur harpist can also do well if prepared and knowledgeable. If you are a beginner or haven't any familiarity with doing weddings, and someone asks you to play for one, it is perfectly permissible to explain your situation, but sometimes the client (or friend, or family member) really wants *you,* and no other harpist will do! In that case, your skill level is not an issue.

BUSINESS

How you do business is what determines how much wedding business you get, of course. Perhaps the single most important factor in how a potential client feels about you is what they hear when they call and get your message machine. If it doesn't sound musical and businesslike, they may hang up. Flippant, silly, or dull greeting messages can be a turn-off to potential clients.

Business cards and brochures are nice to have. Full color, good paper and card stock, and professional layout will represent you well. Spend whatever it takes to get the best. Brochures and business cards with a small plexiglass display stand can be left (with permission) at florist shops and event organizers' offices.

DESCRIBING YOUR HARP

Rates in your area may be different for pedal harpists than for lever harpists. It can be confusing to a bride, who may never have been close to a harp before, to find that there are different kinds of harps, and that the music played on them is not necessarily the same. Being able to accurately describe your harp, its appearance and size, and the music you play, will avoid misunderstanding.

To most people, the word "harp" means a large golden orchestral instrument. Unless someone has specifically said "Celtic" or "Folk" in describing the kind of harp they want, chances are they are assuming yours is a pedal harp.

I make it a point to tell them that mine is a traditional harp, and that it is not large and gold. I do not call my harp "small", since after all, lever harps are generally the same sizes harps have been for many hundreds of years, making them "normal", while pedal harps are a "large", comparatively recent invention, in answer to the growth of the size and volume of orchestras. (see The Harper's Handbook by Laurie Riley for a dateline history of harp development).

No qualitative attitude is appropriate regarding the size of your own harp or anyone else's. All harps are valid and beautiful. The most positive way I know to describe a lever harp is to say, "This is a newly made version of the kind of harp that has been played in weddings for over twelve hundred years".

If you have a photo of yourself with your harp - a full length shot, not a cropped one or a face shot - this will better show your client the size and appearance of your instrument than any amount of description will.

CONTRACTS

Almost every harpist and harper who regularly plays for weddings uses a contract. This avoids surprises. The contract puts your agreement clearly in writing, and keeps everyone happy. People don't always remember verbal agreements accurately. It takes only a few misunderstandings to realize how valuable a contract can be. Over time, you can add details to your contract form as you find them necessary.

The important elements of your contract are:

- Date, time, location, directions, time of arrival and what time you need to leave if you have a time constraint.

- What portions of the ceremony and/or reception you will play for, what pieces you will play, and how long you estimate you will be there, from arrival to departure. Be sure the contract says you will be paid for *actual* time, not *estimated* time.

- Whether you are to be present at the rehearsal, and how long.

- The exact fee for your actual hours, as well as who will pay you and when (i.e., the best man, immediately after the ceremony, or the bride's mother, during the reception).

- Availability of electrical outlets for your amplifier.

- A clause on who is responsible for possible damage to your harp.

- Whether you will play indoors or outdoors, and if outdoors, specify your needs for weather protection and the circumstances in which you will not play (i.e. pouring rain, wind, heavy fog or dew, mud, direct sun, excessive heat, etc).

WHAT TO WEAR

Unless your outfit is your trademark, it's nice to wear something that blends well with the bridal party's clothing. I always ask what color and fabric they will wear, and choose something as similar as possible.

If you're male, the usual choice is white or black. The bigger issue is how formal the wedding is, and this will be the deciding factor in whether you wear a tux, a suit, a sport jacket, or just a nice shirt.

If you are female, having a collection of dresses may seem daunting, and the expense could well run into more than you're paid. However, most bridesmaid's dresses are only worn once; their style is often not in keeping with the tastes of the wearer, and so they end up at consignment and second-hand shops for very affordable prices. One shopping trip to a handful of such shops could result in a collection of good, like-new dresses, one in every color and fabric, for the price of one new one.

Paying attention to how formally the wedding party will be dressed will help you determine your outfit; if you show up formally dressed and the wedding party is in wrinkled linen, you could be embarrassed; likewise, if you're in a cool summer dress and they are in satin and lace, you'll wish you could hide in a corner. Knowing in advance how formally to dress will increase your comfort level.

FOOD

Whether or not you will be expected to partake of any food at the reception is an issue requiring absolute clarity. There are some catering companies which will put a musician on their blacklist if seen eating at a wedding or event (many referrals come through catering companies if they like you). Ask the bride or organizer in advance whether or not you are to join the diners, and if so, have them put that in writing to the caterer. If this is not clarified, assume that eating is not part of your contract, and have a big meal before your arrival.

SELF-SUFFICIENCY

A wedding is the bride's big day, and since most brides are not performers, it may be the only time in her life that she has been the focus of attention of a large group of people. The focus is not on the musician, as it would be at a concert. This means that no one will be making any special effort to see to your needs; you will be expected to function on your own and fit in with the occasion with only the direction you have received prior to the big day. Be sure you have asked all the right questions beforehand. Being aware that you are in the background, you are there for ambience only, will put the event in perspective. Below are two checklists for preparation:

WHAT TO KNOW BEFORE THE WEDDING:

Date
Time
Location
What to play
When to play
How long to play
Who will give you visual cues
Where electrical outlets are
What to wear
When to arrive
When to leave
Where you are to sit
Whether you may eat
How much you will be paid
Who will pay you
When you are to be paid
Whether pay will be cash or check
Whether you are to attend the rehearsal

CHECKLIST

WHAT TO BRING WITH YOU

- **Order of Ceremony** (so you know when to play)

- **List of pieces** (so you know what to play)

- **Notation** (so you know how to play it)

- **Light for harp if necessary** (so you can see your strings)

- **Music stand**

- **Music light** (so you can see your notation)

- **Extension cord** (in case the outlet is too far away for your light cord)

- **Amp** (so you can be heard in larger halls or amid crowds of talking people)

- **Pickup or harp microphone** (so your harp can talk to your amp)

- **Patch Cord** (to connect them to each other)

- **Electronic tuner** (so you can tune when it's noisy)

- **Tuning Key**

- **Extra Strings**

- **String Cutter** (for cutting long ends off new strings)

- **Jeweler's pliers** (for removing old string pieces from soundboard or pins)

- **Stool** (in case there's nothing supplied that is the right height or color)

- **Contract** (to remember accurately what has been agreed upon and to be able to prove it if necessary)

ENJOY!

Most importantly, enjoy yourself. Weddings are fun. Catch the mood. Smile a lot, be friendly. Be celebratory. Answer questions politely. Have a good time. Play beautifully. The experience can often transcend the business and monetary aspects of the event.

PRELUDES

Carolan's Draught

Turlough O'Carolan

(1670 - 1738)

Written by Ireland's legendary composer, Turlough O'Carolan (in Irish, his name was actually Thorbheallbhach Ui Chearbheallan, pronounced: HOR-val-vah oo HAR-va-lan"), who happened to be blind.

He left behind numerous compositions, characterized by the influence of Irish folk music and his love for the popular and exquisite Baroque music of the times. The Baroque influence may be seen in the harmonic texture and the length of each part of the tune, and the structure of the melody may not be as repetitive as in traditional Irish music.

This piece commemorated his love of a good time. It should be played joyfully.

Carolan's Draught

Turlough O'Carolan
(1670-1738)

Theme from 'Jupiter'

Gustav Holst
(1874 - 1934)

This well-known favorite has a magic quality, being solemn and majestic without being too heavy. It is from "The Planets", which includes individual pieces Holst composed to fit what he felt was the character of each planet.

Theme from 'Jupiter'

Gustav Holst
(1874-1934)

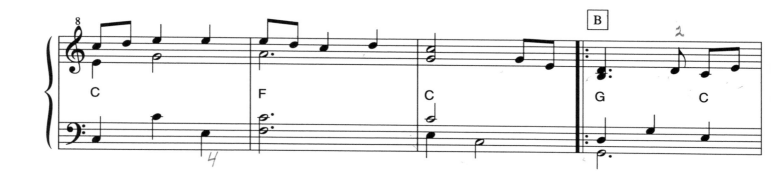

Adaptation and Arrangement © 2000 Beth A. Kollé

Celtic Prelude I

(Kean O'Hara, Third Air)

Turlough O'Carolan

(1670 - 1738)

Although this piece is lovely when played in strict rhythm, it is also effective when played rubato and with expression. Examples of where to linger would be the D chord of measure 4 and the C chord of measure 8, and most obviously at measure 12. Give a good ritard in the last two measures.

Celtic Prelude I

(Kean O'Hara, Third Air)

Turlough O'Carolan
(1670-1738)

With Rubato

Harp

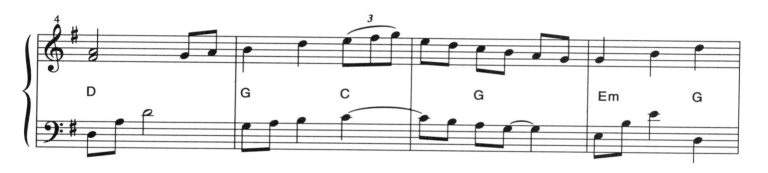

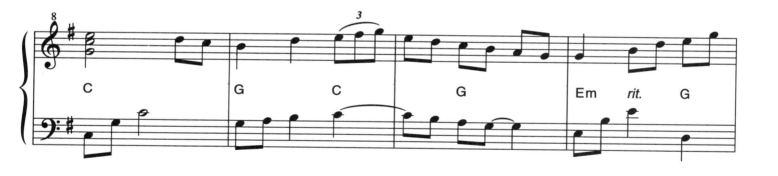

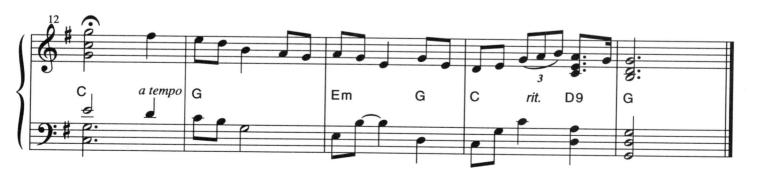

25

Swedish Prelude

(Kringellek från Gagnef)
Traditional Swedish

This Swedish folkdance, pronounced KRING-eh-lek frohn GAHN-yeff, is danced in a circle. Gagnef is a town in the west of Sweden.

The beats are emphasized as follows: ONE-two-THREE, ONE-two-THREE.

The left hand bass ostinato is reminiscent of the drone of the bagpipe, the traditional instrument for this song, while the right hand is free to frolic.

Swedish Prelude

(Kringellek från Gagnef)

Traditional Swedish Folk Melody

27

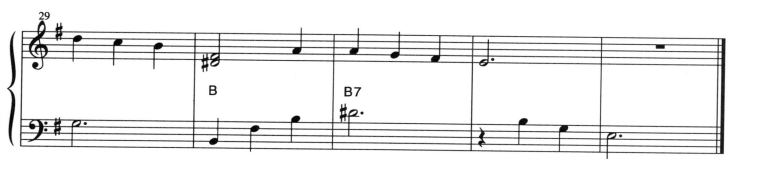

Jewish Wedding Song II

(Zemer Lach)

Traditional Jewish

Sharp the D above middle C for the entire song. The exotic interval between C and D#
gives this old "laughing song" its strong Jewish flavor. The bass hand keeps the beat while
the treble hand syncopates.

Jewish Wedding Song II

(Zemer Lach)

Traditional Jewish Wedding Song

St. Anthony Chorale

Franz Joseph Haydn

(1732 - 1809)

An old favorite, and for good reason. This is a versatile piece which may be played also as a processional at a moderate tempo. The piece may be shortened by eliminating repeats.

St. Anthony Chorale

Joseph Haydn
(1732-1809)

40

PROCESSIONALS

Bridal Chorus

Richard Wagner

(1813 - 1883)

Many brides have dreamed of coming down the aisle to "Here Comes the Bride". It's almost impossible to be too dramatic. However, there are a couple of points to be aware of with this piece.

Most brides tend to scoot down the aisle faster than they're supposed to, so the A part (ending at measure 20) is likely all the harpist needs. If this is a little too short, consider repeating the last phrase of the A part, indicated by the Optional Repeat.

Only if the wedding party is proceeding quite slowly should you launch into the B part, as it changes key and must be resolved by the A-2 section at measure 29.

Bridal Chorus

Richard Wagner
(1813-1883)

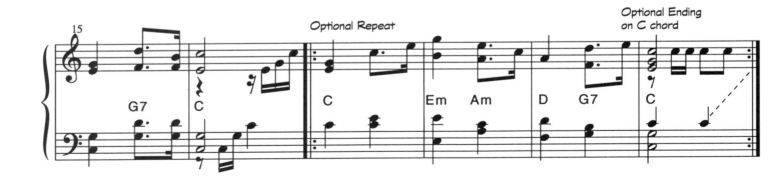

Adaptation and Arrangement © 2000 Beth A. Kollé

Canon in 'D'

Johan Pachelbel

(1653 - 1706)

Pachelbel (pronounced POCK-el-bell) produced much beautiful music in the Baroque period. This is one of the most requested processionals for weddings.

If there is a melody instrument, such as flute or violin, the player may start the melody (starting measure 5) four measures behind the harp.

Because the Canon in D is structured around a short four-measure harmonic scheme, it is perfect for timing the music to fit the wedding party's progress down the aisle. No one has to fidget for long at the end of the procession while the musicians finish playing. Simply conclude the piece at the nearest phrase ending on a D chord or arpeggio.

Cannon in 'D'

J. Pachelbel
(1653-1706)

49

51

Dance of the Blessed Spirits

Christoph W.R. von Gluck

(1714 - 1787)

This elegant piece, appropriate for a formal wedding, lends itself very well to doubling on the flute or violin.

If the procession is short, the first section will suffice. If there are many attendants, it is effective to play the A part, then the B, and continue repeating the B part until the signal is given that the bride is ready to proceed. Allow a brief pause, and then play through the A part to conclude the processional.

Dance of the Blessed Spirits

from 'Orpheus'

C.W.R. von Gluck
(1714-1787)

54

Finale from 'Music for the Royal Fireworks'

George Frideric Handel
(1685 - 1769)

Another old favorite from the Baroque period; the title is, hopefully, not indicative of the future of the marriage.

Finale from 'Music for the Royal Fireworks'

George Frideric Handel
(1685-1759)

Jesu, Joy of Man's Desiring

Johann Sebastian Bach

(1685 - 1750)

Often a favorite with the bride's mother, this piece is a good one to play when requested. Because of its title, it is best to be considerate of the religious affiliation of the family before planning to use it for a wedding.

Be sure to play it rhythmically and evenly for the best effect. A flute or violin doubling the melody is also quite lovely.

Jesu, Joy of Man's Desiring

Johann Sebastian Bach
(1685-1750)

March from 'Scipio'

George Frideric Handel
(1685 - 1759)

A charming addition to the wedding repertoire, this march from the Baroque era offers a refreshing key change to the lever harp repertoire.

March from 'Scipio'

George Frideric Handel
(1685-1759)

CEREMONY / MEDITATIONS

Searching for Lambs

Traditional

This haunting and wistful melody is very effective when used as an introspective interlude during the ceremony - for example, during the lighting of the unity candle.

Searching for Lambs is also an excellent prelude piece. Our suggestion would be to play the piece once as written, repeat an octave higher, and then once again as written.

Take care not to be too strict with the rhythm and tempo; think rubato!

Searching for Lambs

Traditional

Swedish Meditation

(Sollerö Långdans)
Traditional Swedish

A "långdans", or long-dance, like this one from Sollerö, Sweden, is a folkdance performed in a line, with men and women holding hands and proceeding around the floor to the left. (Pronounced SOO-leh-ruh LOHNG-dahns)

Although in ¾ time, the beat is not emphasized in the same way as a waltz. Where a waltz rhythm is played:

ONE-two-three,

the långdans gives more emphasis to the third beat:

ONE-two-THREE, ONE-two-THREE.

Set C♯ as indicated for the duration of the song.

Swedish Meditation

(Sollerö Långdans)

Traditional Swedish Folkdance

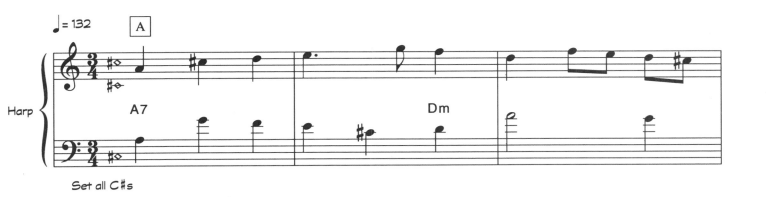

Set all C#s

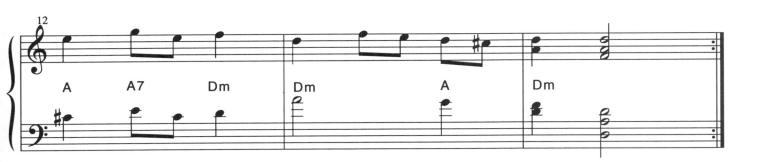

Arrangement © 2000 Beth A. Kollé

Jewish Meditation

(Ma Navu)

Traditional Jewish

A very popular folk dance tune. People might get up and dance if you play it during a reception. It should be played smoothly, with attention to time signature and consistent tempo.

Jewish Meditation

(Ma Navu)

Traditional Jewish Song

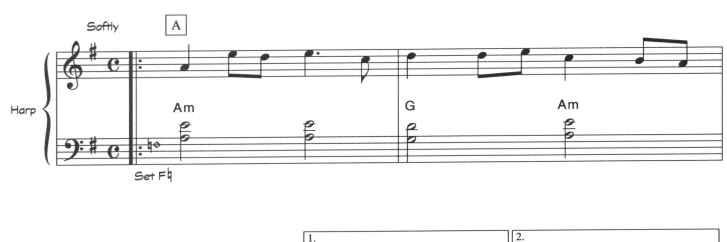

Celtic Meditation

(Eleanor Plunkett)
Turlough O'Carolan
(1670 - 1738)

Written for one of O'Carolan's many patrons, this is one of the loveliest of his compositions. Do not be strict with the tempo, but enjoy each phrase ending before moving on. Provided are grace note ornamentations, and feel free to add some of your own.

Celtic Meditation

(Eleanor Plunkett)

Turlough O'Carolan
(1670-1738)

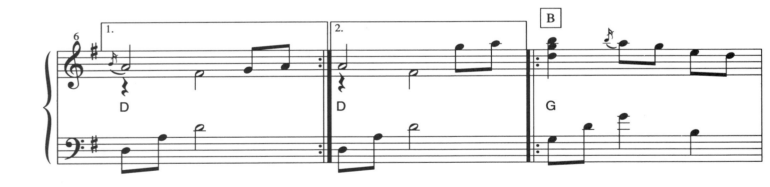

RECESSIONALS

Celtic Recessional 1

(Charles O'Conor)
Turlough O'Carolan
(1670 - 1738)

Another piece written for one of his patrons, this cheerful tune of O'Carolan's should be played in a sprightly, happy fashion. Try playing the 16th notes in the B part by lightly playing alternate fingers, 3-2-1. Practice them slowly first, and then build up speed.

Celtic Recessional I

(Charles O'Conor)

Turlough O'Carolan
(1670-1738)

Celtic Recessional II

(Frank Palmer)
Turlough O'Carolan
(1670-1738)

Similar to Charles O'Conor, also by O'Carolan, this tune is lively even when played at moderate speed. Slight damping in the bass on the eighth-rests of measures 12 – 15 adds to the bouncing rhythm of the piece.

Although no repeats are indicated, feel free to repeat each section as you please.

Celtic Recessional II

(Frank Palmer)

Turlough O'Carolan
(1670-1738)

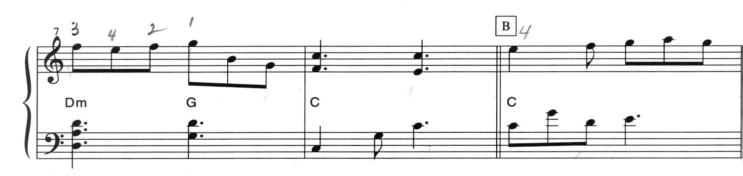

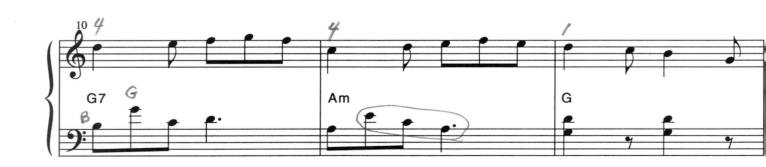

Arrangement © 2000 Beth A. Kollé

88

Celtic Recessional III

(Gilliekrankie)
Traditional

It is likely that this tune was composed by the Irish harper Thomas Connelan, who was living in Scotland in the 1600's. It is well known among Scots.

Try starting the piece at the B part. By playing it this way, the piece has a slightly different character.

Celtic Recessional III

(Gilliekrankie)

Traditional

The Royal Dream

Traditional

A strong French influence, found in much traditional Welsh music, is clearly heard in the lyrical B part of this piece.

Played slowly, The Royal Dream is a good Prelude piece, but it is most exciting when played just after the couple has been introduced as husband and wife. Try playing it the first time up one octave, and then repeating the piece as written.

The Royal Dream

Traditional

94

Trumpet Tune

Henry Purcell
(1659-1695)

This fanfare from the Baroque period will be enjoyed because of its familiarity to many listeners. When played with another instrument doubling the melody, this piece is very festive.

Trumpet Tune

Henry Purc(1659-169

ACKNOWLEDGMENTS

We would like to thank Jack Kollé and Sheri Hargus, our computer advisors.

Brad Spear, a talented flutist, acted as source and consultant for two of the Jewish wedding pieces included in this book.

Susan McLain, a terrific harpist, offered her fine arrangements for our interpretation on Canon in D, Gilliekrankie, Dance of the Blessed Spirits and The Royal Dream.